VMC machine users,
read this book before you buy new VMC
else you will lose upto ₹2.2 Cr profits !

2X YOUR PROFITS FROM VMC

VMC machine users,
read this book before you buy new VMC
else you will lose upto ₹2.2 Cr profits !

2X YOUR PROFITS FROM VMC

SREENIVASULU PATTI

Available on amazonkindle

Worldwide Published by

Pendown Press
PREMIUM BUSINESS PUBLISHER

PENDOWN PRESS LLP

An ISO 9001 & ISO 14001 Certified Co.,

Regd. Office: 3767A, Kanhaiya Nagar,
Tri Nagar, Delhi-110035

Ph.: 8130886000, 9650072927

E-mail: info@pendownpress.com

Branch Office: 1A/2A, 20, Hari Sadan, Ansari Road,
Daryaganj, New Delhi-110002

Ph.: 011-45794768

Website: PendownPress.com

Edition: 2025

Price: ₹ 299

ISBN: 978-93-6338-842-0

Layout and Cover Designed by Pendown Graphics Team

Printed and Bound in India by Thomson Press India Ltd.

Table of Contents

Acknowledgements

First, I would like to thank **my wife, Harsha,** for her support and for allowing me to be who I am, and for helping me on my life journey over the past 23 years. I thank **my daughter, Sanjukta,** for her love. I thank **my parents, Sreeramulu and Sharadha,** for their unconditional love and support throughout my life.

I also want to thank **my mentors, Mr. Rajiv Talreja, Mr. Kiran Hasija, Mr. Akshar Yadav, Mr. Rahul Jain,** and **Mr. Manuj Bajaj,** for inspiring me to write this book.

I cannot miss thanking **my friend Dushyant ji** for guiding me to write this book.

I thank **Dinesh Verma ji** of **Pendown Press** for fine-tuning the manuscript and his team at **@pendown press** for helping me with this book launch. Finally, I thank **Kuvam Technologies Pvt Ltd team member Deepali Paliwal, my Executive Assistant,** for helping me convert the handwritten script to a soft format.

Why This Book?

Manufacturing is the backbone of any economy, and **Small and Medium-sized Enterprises (SMEs)** play a crucial role in driving industrial growth, generating employment, and strengthening exports. However, despite their significance, many SME business owners struggle with manufacturing inefficiencies that lead to **revenue losses, high production costs, and reduced profitability**.

This book intends to spread love, joy, peace, happiness, and abundance, and to serve, guide, and support manufacturing SME business enterprise owners. So that they all have better lives, enjoy more love, experience more joy, and feel more peace and happiness.

One day during a business meeting with my dear customer Late Mr. Kishore Kumar Gupta of Pyn Precision, he was joking with me that after investing Rs.25,00,000/- on a VMC he earns Rs.500/- per hour and a taxi driver earns Rs.1000/- per hour by investing just 5,00,000/- on a taxi.. He had to hire a machine maintenance engineer, cnc programmer, cnc operator, a supervisor, and a manager to manage the show. That conversation moved me such that I felt the need to do something about this, as he was doing great work for ISRO, HAL, and BEL, which are of great importance to our nation. I was compelled to think about what I can do for this industry.

And another day, I had gone to Pune to meet our client, Mr. Gautam, the owner of Pushpak Engineers, and he was telling his friends stories that the margins on VMC machining are going down due to competition.

Despite working for 16 hours a day, they are not able to meet the expenses of the company, like salaries, rent, electricity, etc., and they don't know what to do. After going home, they start consuming alcohol just to remove the pain of running the company. That day, I was shaken from inside, and I decided that I should do something about this industry, which has given me so much.

Inspired by these conversations and situations, I decided to write a book to help them reduce their losses and increase their profits with my 25+ years of machine tool experience as it is the best way to spread this knowledge as I want to reach this to all VMC users who are wasting their resources due to ignorance.

This book is dedicated to helping SME business owners **minimize manufacturing losses and maximize profits**. A well-planned **production strategy on a Vertical Machining Center** (**VMC**) can be a game-changer for any business, regardless of the industry.

The right approach to machining can:

- **Enhance efficiency**
- Improve return on investment (ROI)
- Increase production output
- **And reduce waste.**

Who Am I & Why Should You Even Read What I Write?

My name is **Sreenivasulu Patti**, and my company specializes in **CNC Rotary Tables, Angle Heads, and Tilting Rotary Tables.**

I was born into a simple yet deeply values-driven family. My father, a First Divisional Clerk in the Karnataka government, was the sole breadwinner. We were four siblings, and I was the youngest. My mother dedicated herself to raising us with love and discipline. Despite financial constraints, my parents ensured that education remained our top priority. Their sacrifices and unwavering belief in the power of knowledge helped all four of us earn post-graduation degrees, a testament to their commitment to our future.

Money was always in short supply. With just one earning member and the high cost of higher education, we often faced financial struggles. Growing up, I was determined to change this. I dreamt of becoming successful and ensuring my family never had to worry about money again.

One day, I heard someone say, **"Engineers and Doctors make a lot of money and can become very rich."** That statement stuck with me. With a burning desire to improve our lives, I worked relentlessly to secure an engineering admission on merit through sheer dedication. In those days, there were very few engineering colleges, and limited seats were available. If one wanted a seat on general merit, one needed to get an all-Karnataka ranking within 2600 out of a million students. I got admission into Karnataka

University, Vishweshwaraih Engineering College, Bagalkot, and I completed my Mechanical Engineering degree with distinction in 1996.

The First Steps into the Corporate World

My professional journey began in 1996 as a sales engineer with a humble salary in Bangalore. Though the amount was small, my ambition was not.

In 1998, I got an opportunity to work in New Delhi as an assistant Regional Manager, eager to take on bigger responsibilities and challenges. Side by side, I did an MBA in marketing and finance while working.

I got trained thoroughly at various prestigious organizations across the globe, such as, Thomson Industries-Singapore, Bosch Rexroth-Germany, R+W-Germany, HSD-Italy and China, Rosa Grinding Machines, Italy, TBI-Taiwan, Cells Tec- Taiwan, Chandox-Taiwan, Rotoflux-Italy, Gifu, Taiwan, UCAM Bengalore.

Over the next 20 years, through relentless hard work, perseverance, and an unquenchable thirst for learning, I climbed the corporate ladder and eventually reached the highest level in the company as **a Business Head.**

Despite the success, something inside me kept pushing for more. I wanted to create a larger impact, to go beyond personal achievements, and contribute to the nation's progress by generating jobs and opportunities for others.

That thought ignited my entrepreneurial dream.

The First Attempt – A Hard Lesson Learned

In 2010, I took the bold step of starting my own business. I was filled with passion, but I lacked something equally crucial—

experience and business knowledge. As a result, my first venture faced financial challenges and, unfortunately,I had to shut down its operations.

Running out of money was a harsh reality check, but it also became my greatest teacher.

Failures can either break you or shape you. I chose the latter.

The Comeback – Rising Stronger

After years of reflection, learning, and preparation, I decided to restart my entrepreneurial journey in 2017. This time, I was armed with experience, better financial planning, and a deeper understanding of business dynamics.

The road was not easy, but persistence paid off. By 2017, I had started with just one employee, and today, we have grown into a **strong team of 40+ members**—working together, building something meaningful, and making a real impact.

The Journey Continues…

Looking back, my journey has been one of resilience, learning, and constant growth. From a meagre salary to leading a successful business, from corporate leadership to entrepreneurship, every step has been filled with challenges, but also invaluable lessons.

Today, my mission is to see everyone around me living in love and joy, being happy and peaceful, and having gratitude and compassion. Not just personal success but also creating opportunities for others, contributing to the economy, and proving that with determination, nothing is impossible. This is just the beginning. The journey continues…

Why Am I Sharing This Knowledge & What To Expect From This Book?

My passion for machining began over **29 years ago** when I started my career as a sales engineer. From the very beginning, I was fascinated by how **small improvements in machining strategies could create massive impacts on production efficiency and profitability**. I have worked with **hundreds of machine manufacturers and thousands of SME business owners**, helping them optimize their machining processes, reduce losses, and **increase their bottom line**.

You may wonder, **why am I writing this book when this knowledge could be sold as a premium course or consultation?**

There are two key reasons:

1. **A Deep Passion for the Machine Tool Industry!**

   I have spent my entire career working with **SME manufacturers**, and it pains me to see how many businesses **struggle due to a lack of knowledge** about VMC optimization. **More than 50% of machine investments go to waste** due to **poor machining strategies, inefficient setups, and a lack of process planning**. If these businesses are not guided properly, they risk losing **crores of rupees** in revenue. Through this book, I want to put as many SME business owners as possible on the **right path** and help them **prevent unnecessary losses** and bring love, joy, peace, and happiness into their lives.

2. **Time Constraints**

   The second reason is a lack of time; while I would love to **personally guide every SME business owner**, it is not always possible due to time limitations. This book serves as my **gift to small business owners and startups**, where I share **10 valuable lessons** that I have learned throughout my journey as a machining expert.

By applying the strategies in this book, you will be able to improve your manufacturing efficiency, reduce losses, and significantly increase your profits.

What to Expect?

This book is designed to provide **practical, easy-to-implement strategies for VMC users.**

If You are a:

- **SME and large business owners with VMC and HMC machines**
- **Machine shop owner,**
- **Manufacturing entrepreneur**
- Production managers

This book is for you.

Within the pages of this book, you will learn how to easily:

- Reduce machining inefficiencies and production losses.
- Optimize tool usage and cycle times.
- Improve component accuracy and reduce rejection rates.
- Enhance machine utilization and increase ROI.
- Scale production without heavy investments.

The journey so far has been **incredible**, and I look forward to sharing my knowledge with you. I am certain that the lessons shared in this book will help you **unlock the true potential of your machining setup** and take your business to the next level.

Here's to **higher profits, smarter machining, and a thriving manufacturing business!**

Your friendly machining expert,

Sreenivasulu Patti

CHAPTER 1

Preventing Machine Breakdowns: Maximizing VMC Longevity & Efficiency

Machine breakdowns are one of the biggest sources of losses in manufacturing.

With my 25+ years of experience in the machine tool industry, I have identified that the number one reason for these breakdowns is not following the manufacturer's guidelines while selecting and operating a VMC.

While buying a new VMC, proper selection of specifications is very important, especially on spindle speed and XYZ axes strokes.

If it is for a production job, a slower rpm spindle, i.e, 6000, needs to be selected. If it is for a die and mold, pattern-making machine spindle rpm should be above 6000, with a chiller should be selected. Based on the component size and fixture size machine table size and strokes should be selected. If the fixture height is higher, a column raiser must be selected.

If the selection of machine specifications is wrong, then the breakdowns and losses will increase.

When a machine breaks down, it creates a chain reaction of inefficiencies:

- Operators sit idle, waiting for repairs to be completed.
- If the component needs to be processed on another machine, the production flow is disrupted.
- A ripple effect occurs, where multiple machines may need to be stopped due to a single machine breakdown.

Proactive Measures to Reduce Machine Breakdowns

To prevent machine failures and extend the lifespan of your VMC, consider implementing the following best practices:

- **First-Run Idle Cycle:** Before beginning production each day, run an idle cycle where all axes move through their full strokes. This allows the ball screw and LM guide to receive proper lubrication, which significantly reduces wear and tear and increases the machine's lifespan.
- **Managing Heat Generation in High-Speed Applications:** If your VMC operates above 5000 RPM (especially in die and mold applications), prolonged cycle times can cause excessive heat buildup.

  This heat is transferred to the:

  - **Spindle:** Leading to overheating and premature bearing failure.
  - **LM Guides & Ball Screws:** Resulting in thermal expansion and accelerated wear.
  - **Machine Structure:** Causing inaccuracies and misalignment over time.

How to Prevent Overheating & Minimize Wear & Tear

- **Use Spindle Cooling Systems:** Investing in a spindle cooling system can dissipate excess heat and prevent thermal expansion from affecting machining accuracy. It increases the spindle life, LM guide life and ball screw life which are the main parts of the machine.
- **Reduce Spindle Load** and increase spindle life

Smart Maintenance = Higher Productivity

By following manufacturer guidelines, implementing preventive maintenance, and using intelligent machining accessories, you can:

- Reduce machine downtime
- Lower maintenance costs
- Extend VMC lifespan
- Enhance production efficiency

A well-maintained machine is a profitable machine!

Investing in the right VMC and with proactive maintenance, your VMC will deliver consistent performance for years to come.

CHAPTER 2

Maximizing VMC Productivity by Reducing Tool Change Time

A Client Case Study

The Background, The Client & The Concern

I met Mr. Rajesh at a business meeting in a big MNC. He was under pressure from his Director to increase the production of auto components in his department. He had heard about me through his friend that we help manufacturers in reducing losses and increasing profits without adding new machines. He asked us for a technical consultation on reducing their component cycle time.

The Study & Discovery

I visited their company to study their machining process. When they were machining a component, they often needed to use **multiple cutting** tools depending on the operations involved—drilling, milling, tapping, etc.

However, every time the machine changes a tool, it stops machining for 4 seconds, leading to a significant loss of productive time.

The Hidden Loss: Tool Change Downtime

- Each tool change takes **4 seconds.**
- If you change tools **1,000 times per day,** you lose **4,000 seconds** (over **66 minutes of idle time**).
- This is the time when their machine was **not cutting, not producing, and not generating any revenue.**

> **Now, imagine a scenario where you could reduce the number of tool changes without affecting production quality. This is where smart batch machining strategies come into play.**

The Proposed Solution: Load Multiple Components & Optimize Tool Usage

Instead of machining **one component at a time and changing tools frequently,** a more efficient strategy is to:

- Load multiple components onto the worktable at once.
- Using quick change fixtures with zero point clamping system with multiple fixtures. This will reduce the component loading and unloading time, fixture changing time and set up time.
- Use the same tool on all components before switching to the next tool.
- Continue this process for all tools, reducing unnecessary tool changes.
- Our study revealed that selecting combination tools like drilling and chamfering in the same tool can reduce the number of tools, tool holders, and tool changing time.

when you reduce tool changes, power consumption goes down, improves ball screw and LM guide life due to less axes movements

Why This Works

Smarter Tool Management = More Productivity

- **Fewer Tool Changes = Less Downtime:** Instead of changing tools 1,000 times a day, you might only change them 250 times, reducing wasted time significantly.
- **More Machining, Less Waiting:** The spindle spends more time cutting metal instead of idling.
- **Higher Productivity & Faster Output:** Your VMC can produce more parts in the same working hours.
- **Lower Wear & Tear:** Reducing frequent tool changes can extend automatic tool changer life and reduce wear on the tool changer mechanism.

Key Takeaway: Small Change, Big Impact

By implementing batch machining, using combination tools, and strategic tool sequencing, you can increase VMC productivity without additional investment.

- This simple yet highly effective approach can lead to:
- More parts produced per shift
- Lower machine idle time
- Higher overall efficiency

In manufacturing, every second counts. Optimizing tool change frequency **is one of the simplest ways** to reduce waste, increase efficiency, and boost profits.

Worksheet to Calculate Time Losses in the Process

1. **OP 10**

   A. Machining time

   B. Tool change time

   C. Number of tool changes

   D. Loading and unloading time

   E. Set up change time

2. **OP 20**

   A. Machining time

   B. Tool change time

   C. Number of tool changes

   D. Loading and unloading time

   E. Set up change time

3. **OP 30**

   A. Machining time

   B. Tool change time

   C. Number of tool changes

   D. Loading and unloading time

   E. Set up change time

4. **OP 40**

   A. Machining time

   B. Tool change time

   C. Number of tool changes

   D. Loading and unloading time

   E. Set up change time

Total cycle time

Potential time reduction

Add up all loading, unloading time, set up time, and tool change time if you use the same tools in OP10, OP20, OP 30, OP 40 etc

CHAPTER 3

Helping an Auto Component Manufacturer Boost Production by 50%

In the last chapter, I explained the importance of selecting the right VMC, and proactive maintenance of VMC is a game-changer. In this chapter, I will cover how simple manufacturing strategies can reduce losses up to 50%!

In a business seminar, I met Mr. Vijay (name changed due to NDA), and during the discussions, he explained to me that they are into manufacturing automobile pistons, a critical auto component.

He was in pain from losses in business, despite giving 14 to 16 hours of time daily to his business. He was facing problems of employee absenteeism, low productivity, and low profit margins in the business.

He requested that I help him increase their production of components without adding new machines, as he was not inclined to take on more debt. He invited me to visit their plant to study their processes and provide advice for reducing losses.

The machining process involved three different faces machining, and to complete all the operations, they had set up three separate fixtures, one for each side machining step. The same component was made on 3 different machines. One side machining on one machine and then moving to the next 2 machines for the other 2 sides.

If one machine operator was absent, the other two machines were affected because of the lack of an input component.

After every operation, their team had to:

- Stop the machine
- Unclamp and unload the component
- Clean both the component and the fixture
- Move the component to the next fixture and repeat the process
- Load a new work piece

Each of these changeovers took 1 to 2 minutes, leading to significant downtime. Imagine that for every 2 minutes of machining time, there was a wastage of 1 to 2 minutes.

When you are producing 1000's of components, this loss becomes very significant.

The Problem: High Costs and Wastage

The company was facing multiple challenges:

- **Inefficiency:** The repeated loading and unloading process consumed unnecessary time.
- **High Fixture Costs:** Instead of one, they were investing in three fixtures, tripling their costs.
- **Rework and Waste:** If a component failed at the second

fixture, all previous machining efforts were wasted.

- **Low Production Output:** Due to excessive handling, their production rate was much lower than their potential.
- **Absenteeism:** Team members were taking unplanned leaves and causing considerable downtime of the machine

Frustrated by low productivity and high rejection rates, Mr. Vijay requested a solution.

After carefully analyzing their process, we recommended installing a **CNC rotary table** on their **VMC (Vertical Machining Center).**

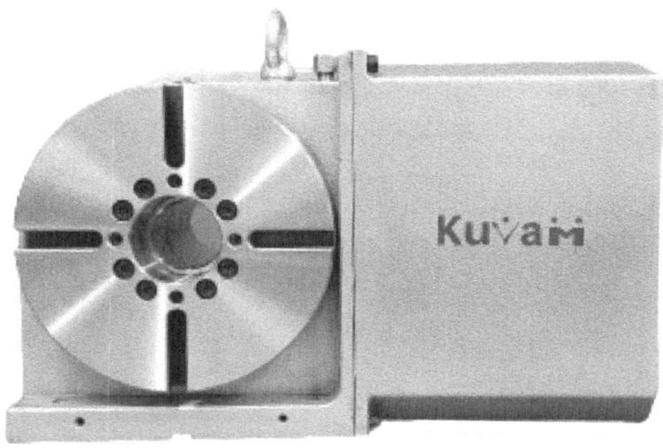

This allowed them to:

- Load the component once
- Index (rotate) it to the required position automatically
- Machine all three faces in a **single setup**

The Results

- **50% Increase in Production Capacity**: Fewer interruptions meant faster cycle times.

- **Eliminated Fixture Inaccuracies**: No more misalignment issues between fixtures.
- **Saved Two Fixtures:** Reducing unnecessary fixture costs.
- **Reduced Downtime**: Reduced unloading and reloading of components between operations.

This transformation helped Mr. Vijay's company maximize efficiency, reduce costs, and significantly improve product quality.

Since the cycle time goes up, the operator becomes free to operate a second machine or do component inspection. Thus reducing the requirement for more manpower.

Worksheet to Calculate Time Losses in the Process

1. **OP 10**

    F. Machining time

    G. Tool change time

    H. Number of tool changes

    I. Loading and unloading time

    J. Set up change time

2. **OP 20**

    F. Machining time

    G. Tool change time

    H. Number of tool changes

    I. Loading and unloading time

    J. Set up change time

3. **OP 30**

    F. Machining time

    G. Tool change time

    H. Number of tool changes

    I. Loading and unloading time

    J. Set up change time

4. **OP 40**

    F. Machining time

G. Tool change time

H. Number of tool changes

I. Loading and unloading time

J. Set up change time

Total cycle time

Potential time reduction

Add up all loading, unloading time, set up time, and tool change time if you use the same tools in OP10, OP20, OP 30, OP 40 etc

CHAPTER 4

Scaling Up

A few days after implementing the CNC rotary table, tasting the breakthrough in increasing VMC productivity, Mr. Vijay approached us again with a new challenge:

He asked, "Can we further increase productivity on the same machine? Customer demand has gone up!". His condition was the same; he still didn't want to add new VMCs as it would require him to hire 3 more CNC machine operators, increase power requirements, and more space on the shop floor.

Identifying Further Improvements

We revisited their process, analyzing where more time savings could be achieved. Our study revealed that significant time was being lost in:

- **Tool change time**
- **Component unloading and loading**
- **Machine axes movements**

We recommended upgrading to a **CNC rotary production system** that allowed them to load **four components simultaneously instead of one.**

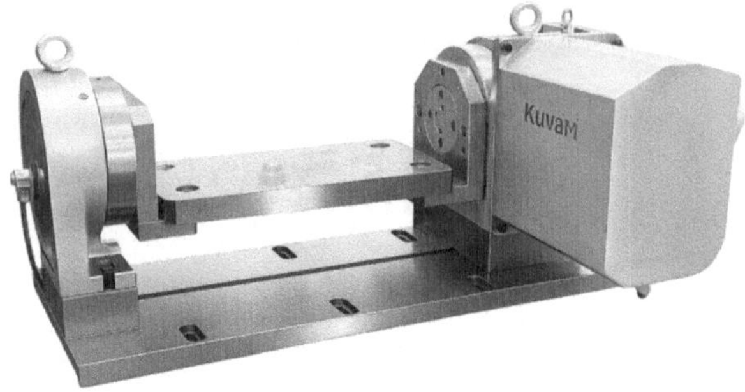

A CNC rotary production system is nothing but a CNC rotary table with trunnion support and a cradle fixture to accommodate a larger number of components with double load carrying capacity.

This optimization led to:

- **Reduced Tool Change Delays**: The machine continued cutting for a longer period before stopping.
- **Less Machine Downtime**: Instead of stopping the machine **four times,** they now stop **it only once per cycle.**

Additional Optimization: Manpower Efficiency

With this improvement, the cycle time increased, leading to the operator standing idle during machining.

To maximize efficiency, we suggested that one operator manage two machines instead of one, cutting manpower costs by 50%.

The Results

- **Doubled Production Output:** Meeting the increased customer demand.
- **50% Reduction in Manpower Requirement:** Lower labor costs.
- **Optimized Machine Utilization:** Less idle time, more productivity.

> By implementing these changes, Mr. Vijay's company was able to scale up production without investing in a new machine, making their existing setup more profitable and efficient.

Worksheet to Calculate Time Losses in the Process

1. **OP 10**

   K. Machining time

   L. Tool change time

   M. Number of tool changes

   N. Loading and unloading time

   O. Set up change time

2. **OP 20**

   K. Machining time

   L. Tool change time

   M. Number of tool changes

   N. Loading and unloading time

   O. Set up change time

3. **OP 30**

   K. Machining time

   L. Tool change time

   M. Number of tool changes

   N. Loading and unloading time

   O. Set up change time

4. **OP 40**

   K. Machining time

L. Tool change time

M. Number of tool changes

N. Loading and unloading time

O. Set up change time

Total cycle time

Potential time reduction

Add up all loading, unloading time, set up time, and tool change time if you use the same tools in OP10, OP20, OP 30, OP 40 etc

CHAPTER 5

A Simple Strategy Revolutionized Orthopedic Implant Manufacturing

A Client Case Study

The Background

I had gone to an international business seminar where I met Mr. Arora. When I explained, my mission is to help SME business owners in reducing their manufacturing losses and increasing their profits, and bringing love, joy, peace, and happiness to their lives. He wanted me to help him increase their production capacity.

The Client

Mr. Arora was an orthopedic implant manufacturer with 12 years of manufacturing experience. He had undertaken several training programs and was always focused on increasing sales. He had even hired a consultant to help him increase their production. He had tried all the options that he knew about. Having tried numerous options without satisfactory results, he was tired and wary of trying anything new.

He was facing serious challenges in producing **screw plates,**—a critical medical component designed to support fractured bones. Orthopedic implants are used to join broken bones. His manufacturing setup included a **Vertical Machining Center (VMC) with only 3 axes**, which posed a major limitation. Since orthopedic implants must be tailored to match the natural curvature of a patient's bone, machining them requires **precise angular adjustments.**

The Problem: Manual Adjustments, Programmer Dependency & Downtime

Despite having a high-end ₹30-lakh CNC machine, Mr. Arora's team struggled with inefficiencies due to:

- **Limited Machine Capabilities:** The 3-axis setup wasn't equipped to handle the required angular changes smoothly. Adjustments had to be made **manually using custom-built fixtures, leading to errors and inconsistencies.**
- **Time-Consuming Manual Fixtures:** The team relied on **adjustable manual fixtures** to set the angle for each implant. Every time the implant angle changed, they had to manually reposition the fixture, which was both tedious and imprecise.
- **High Dependence on Skilled CNC Programmers:** Since each component required a different machining angle, a **highly skilled CNC programmer** had to tweak the machine program frequently. If the programmer was unavailable or out of town, the **entire production line came to a halt,** leaving the expensive CNC machine idle and generating zero revenue.

- **Frequent Setup Changes & Wasted Time:** Setting up the fixture for each implant consumed **significant time,** delaying production and increasing lead times. Since each setup was different, operators had to be extra cautious, leading to slow production speeds.

> The company was losing both time and money, with frequent machine downtime, rework due to inaccuracies, and unnecessary delays in production. Frustrated with these limitations, Mr. Arora approached us, seeking a solution that could help him manufacture orthopedic implants efficiently using his existing VMC.

The Solution: CNC Tilting Rotary Table

After conducting an in-depth study of their machining process, **we recommended integrating a CNC tilting rotary table into their VMC. This upgrade provided 4th and 5th-axis capabilities, enabling them to:**

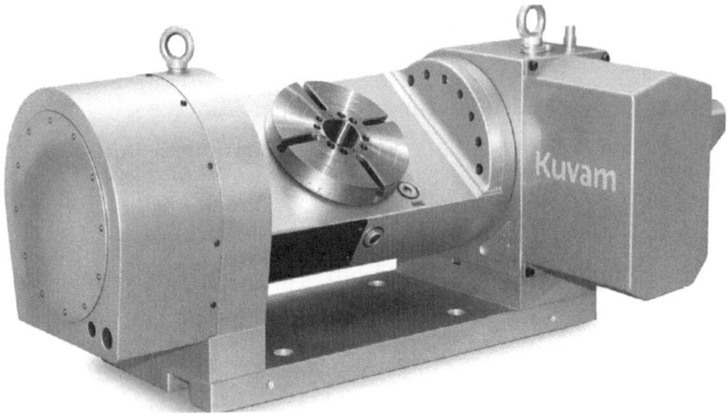

- **Eliminate Multiple Manual Fixtures:** The tilting rotary table allowed seamless angle adjustments without the need for multiple custom fixtures, reducing setup complexity.
- **Achieve Precise Angular Machining:** The tilting and rotating capabilities of the table allowed the machine to cut at precise angles, ensuring consistency and accuracy.
- **Reduce Dependency on CNC Programmers:** Since the rotary table could automatically adjust angles, there was far less need for frequent reprogramming. Operators could run the machine efficiently without waiting for a programmer.
- **Improve Accuracy & Reduce Rejections:** With a **computer-controlled tilting mechanism**, each implant was machined with **high precision**, eliminating human errors associated with manual fixture adjustments.
- **Increase Productivity & Minimize Downtime:** By **automating angle adjustments**, the production process became much smoother, reducing idle time and boosting overall efficiency.

The Results: A 3X Increase in Production & Zero Downtime

By implementing the CNC tilting rotary table, Mr. Arora's company transformed its manufacturing process and achieved:

- **300% Increase in Production Output:** The improved workflow enabled them to produce **three times more implants** within the same timeframe.
- **Eliminated Costly Machine Downtime:** The ₹30-lakh CNC machine was now fully utilized, ensuring maximum return on investment (ROI).
- **Higher Accuracy, Lower Rejections: The automated angle adjustments resulted in** flawless machining, reducing rejections **and improving overall product quality.**
- **Faster Changeovers & More Flexibility:** Switching between different implant designs became effortless, allowing them to take on more custom orders without delay.

The Takeaway: A Game-Changer for Orthopedic Manufacturing

With this simple yet powerful upgrade, Mr. Arora's company overcame its **manufacturing bottlenecks, reduced costs, and significantly increased production efficiency**. The CNC tilting rotary table turned their **3-axis VMC into a powerful, high-precision 5-axis machining system**, enabling them to meet growing demand while ensuring product consistency.

This case study highlights how the right CNC accessory can transform a business, maximize machine potential, and boost profitability, all without the need for costly new machine purchases.

Worksheet to Calculate Time Losses in the Process

1. **OP 10**

    K. Machining time

    L. Tool change time

    M. Number of tool changes

    N. Loading and unloading time

    O. Set up change time

2. **OP 20**

    K. Machining time

    L. Tool change time

    M. Number of tool changes

    N. Loading and unloading time

    O. Set up change time

3. **OP 30**

    K. Machining time

    L. Tool change time

    M. Number of tool changes

    N. Loading and unloading time

    O. Set up change time

4. **OP 40**

    K. Machining time

L. Tool change time

M. Number of tool changes

N. Loading and unloading time

O. Set up change time

Total cycle time

Potential time reduction

Add up all loading, unloading time, set up time, and tool change time if you use the same tools in OP10, OP20, OP 30, OP 40 etc

CHAPTER 6

An Angle Head Turned a VMC into an HMC in Seconds

A Client Case Study

The Client

Mr. Kunal had seen our blogs on the internet, and he approached us to reduce the cycle time in producing their big printing machine component.

The Problem: The Need for an HMC Without the Investment

He faced a persistent challenge in **side machining** on their components. Their existing **Vertical Machining Center (VMC)** was not equipped to handle side operations efficiently, leading to:

- **Lengthy Setup Time:** Every time they needed to perform side machining, they had to stop the machine, manually reposition the component, and set up new fixtures. They were unable to install a CNC Rotary table as it could not accommodate their big component because of space constraints.

This process consumed significant time and affected productivity.

Another option was to send his component to another vendor for side machining on an HMC (horizontal machining centre). If the vendor was busy with other material production, he had to wait till their turn came. Waiting time was causing business loss as opportunities were slipping away from his hands.

- **Component Rejections:** Due to multiple setups, slight misalignments between operations led to inaccuracies, causing high rejection rates.

Frustrated with delays and production inefficiencies, they approached us for a technical consultation to find a solution that could optimize their machining process.

Ideally, the customer needed a **Horizontal Machining Center (HMC)** to perform side machining without additional setups. However, purchasing an **HMC was a huge investment**, and they wanted to explore solutions that could help them achieve the same functionality **using their existing VMC**.

The Solution: Angle Head Integration

After a thorough study of their component and machining process, **we recommended integrating an Angle Head into their VMC.**

This simple yet effective upgrade allowed them to:

- **Perform Side Machining in a Single Setup:** The angle head eliminated the need to stop the machine and manually reposition the component, drastically reducing setup time.

- **Convert Their VMC into an HMC in Seconds:** With the angle head attachment, their existing VMC could perform horizontal machining operations just like an HMC, without the need for an expensive machine upgrade.
- **Eliminate Fixture Changes & Setup Errors:** Since the machining was now done in a single setup, there were no fixture misalignments, improving accuracy and reducing rejection rates.
- **Seamlessly Integrate into the Tool Magazine:** The angle head was stored in the machine's tool magazine, allowing automatic tool changes whenever needed, without any manual intervention.

The Results: Faster Production, Zero Rejections, No HMC Investment

By implementing the angle head, the customer achieved:

- **Drastically Reduced Setup Time:** No more stopping the machine to reposition the component. Machining was done in a single setup, **saving hours of production time**.
- **100% Accuracy & Zero Rejections:** Eliminating fixture misalignment led to consistent machining results, significantly **reducing rework and scrap rates**.
- **Increased Productivity:** With quicker tool changes and uninterrupted machining, they **produced more components in less time**.
- **Massive Cost Savings:** Instead of investing in a **costly HMC**, they **achieved the same functionality** on their existing VMC with a simple, affordable **angle head attachment**.

The Takeaway: A Simple Upgrade That Made a Huge Impact

> This case study demonstrates how a small yet strategic investment in an angle head can maximize a VMC's capabilities, eliminate extra setups, and significantly boost productivity, without spending crores on a new HMC.

By optimizing their process, our customer not only increased efficiency and profitability but also gained a competitive edge in the market, all thanks to a simple but powerful angle head integration.

Worksheet to Calculate Time Losses in the Process

1. **OP 10**

   P. Machining time

   Q. Tool change time

   R. Number of tool changes

   S. Loading and unloading time

   T. Set up change time

2. **OP 20**

   P. Machining time

   Q. Tool change time

   R. Number of tool changes

   S. Loading and unloading time

   T. Set up change time

3. **OP 30**

   P. Machining time

   Q. Tool change time

   R. Number of tool changes

   S. Loading and unloading time

T. Set up change time

4. **OP 40**

P. Machining time

Q. Tool change time

R. Number of tool changes

S. Loading and unloading time

T. Set up change time

Total cycle time

Potential time reduction

Add up all loading, unloading time, set up time, and tool change time if you use the same tools in OP10, OP20, OP 30, OP 40 etc

CHAPTER 7

Maximizing Workforce Efficiency with 4thAxis CNC Rotary Tables

A Client Case Study

The Client & The Concern

Mr. Shashank had heard about us through his friend Pankaj, who told him that they have increased production capacity by 50% without adding new machines. He had advised him to contact us for their manufacturing challenges.

Mr. Shashank invited me to visit their plant and help him increase his production capacity without increasing investments in new machines.

The Worrisome Situation

He had several VMC machines. He was always under pressure to add new machines whenever new orders came. He had to apply for more power connections. So he was not enjoying the production pressures he was getting from his customers..

He told me he was making more money in real estate investments rather than his business, compared to the money, time, and effort he was spending. But he wanted to carry on this business as his father had built his company with lots of passion, and he wanted to grow it.

When he installed a **new 3-axis Vertical Machining Center (VMC)**, he was typically required to hire new **2 to 3 CNC operators**, depending on whether he ran the machine in **an 8-hour or 12-hour shift**.

As his production expanded and he was installing new **VMCs**, the number of required operators increased proportionally.

- **2 VMCs = 4 to 6 machine operators**
- **4 VMCs = 8 to 12 machine operators**

This direct increase in manpower requirements adds to his **labor costs, training expenses, and overall operational complexity**. But the problem was that the CNC operator's absenteeism was hurting his business and resulting in production loss.

The Smart Solution

Then we explained to him that there is a smarter way to **increase production without increasing labor costs**—by **installing a 4th Axis CNC Rotary Table or a production system.**

We integrated a **4th Axis CNC production Rotary Table with their VMC** and **doubled the output** of a single machine:

- ➢ **One machine can now handle the workload of two VMCs.**
- ➢ **Fewer machine operators were needed,** reducing their manpower requirements by **50%.**
- ➢ **Eliminated their need for multiple setups,** reducing time

spent on manual repositioning and fixture changes.

- **Improved accuracy and consistency,** reducing rework and scrap rates.
- **Reduced power requirement and space requirement.** In bigger cities, space comes at a very high cost. Now he does not have to apply for a new power connection.

The Cost-Saving Impact

Let's consider a scenario where his manufacturing unit operates with **six 3-axis VMCs**, requiring **12 operators**. By upgrading each machine with a **4th-axis rotary production table**, the company can:

- Reduce the number of machines required from **6 to 3** while maintaining the same production levels.
- Cut the number of operators needed from **12 to just 6**, leading to a **50% reduction in labor costs.**
- Free up floor space, reducing factory congestion and improving workflow efficiency.

Key Takeaway: Invest in Smart Automation

Instead of hiring more operators or purchasing additional machines, investing in a CNC rotary table can be a cost-effective solution that significantly enhances production efficiency. This allows SME manufacturers to remain competitive, profitable, and scalable without incurring excessive overhead costs.

More output with fewer machines and operators =

Higher profitability!

He was very happy with our solution after trying it on one machine, now he has requested us to replicate the same on another 4 machines.

CHAPTER 8

Optimizing Factory Space & Investment

A Client Case Study

The Client & The Concern

Mr. Raju, a close friend of mine, had started a new business venture in manufacturing precision components. Our friendship was almost 20 years old. He had lots of business opportunities, and he required new machines.

His challenge was space. Gurugram, being a posh city, the cost of land was very expensive.

When he **installed** a new 3-axis Vertical Machining Center (VMC), it occupied a floor space of @100 sq ft in his factory and consumed a 25 KVA power connection. Whenever production demand increased, he opted to install a second VMC, leading to:

- Double the space requirement
- Double the installed power consumption
- Double the capital investment in machinery

While this approach looked like the only way to scale up production, it was putting too much stress on the company's finances as the loan amount was going up and putting pressure on the profitability. Then he discussed whether there is a smarter and more cost-effective alternative option.

I advised him to upgrade their existing VMCs with the CNC Rotary Production System after looking at his components.

By integrating 4th-axis rotary solutions, he doubled the production capacity on the same VMC, eliminating the need for an additional machine.

This resulted in:

- Higher productivity without additional machines
- Significant space savings in your factory
- Lower electricity consumption and operating costs
- Reduced capital investment in new VMCs

The Financial & Operational Benefits

- Cost Savings on Capital Investment – Instead of spending ₹30–₹40 lakhs on a second VMC, he invested a fraction of that amount in a CNC rotary table to achieve the same production output.
- **Optimized Factory Space:** Factory space is a premium resource. He avoided unnecessary expansion costs by maximizing the efficiency of existing machines.
- **Lower Power Consumption:** A second VMC means an additional power load and energy expenses. By enhancing the current setup, he saved on long-term electricity costs.

- **Better Accuracy & Quality:** Multi-axis machining allowed for fewer setups, fewer errors, and greater precision, resulting in higher-quality finished components.

Key Takeaways: Smarter Scaling, Higher Profits

Rather than buying additional machines, they smartly invested in CNC rotary production systems and maximized their current resources.

This strategy ensured him:

- Higher production output
- Lower capital investment
- Reduced power & space requirements
- Better factory utilization

> By making intelligent investments in machining automation, **he increased profitability without expanding the factory footprint and the unnecessary costs on human resources and power connections!**

CHAPTER 9

Optimizing Serration Machining: A Game-Changer for Productivity

The Client & The Challenge

Mr. Khurana, one of our customers, was struggling with long cycle times and high tool breakages while making serrations in steel components. The existing process, which relied on a small end mill, was slow and inefficient, making it difficult to meet his production targets.

Frustrated with the bottlenecks in production, he approached us for a solution to reduce cycle time and improve overall efficiency.

Our Solution: Upgrading the Tooling Strategy

After conducting a detailed study of their machining process, we identified two key inefficiencies:

- **Use of a Small End Mill:** The tool's limited cutting capability led to long machining times and frequent tool wear, increasing costs.
- **Standard Vertical Approach:** The existing VMC setup required multiple passes to complete the serration, slowing down production.

To overcome these challenges, we suggested:

- **Switching to a Cutter:** By replacing the small end mill with a more efficient cutter, material removal became faster and more aggressive, significantly reducing cycle time.
- **Using a 90° Angular Head:** Integrating an angular head allowed them to machine the serration from the side rather than from the top, enabling faster and more precise cutting.

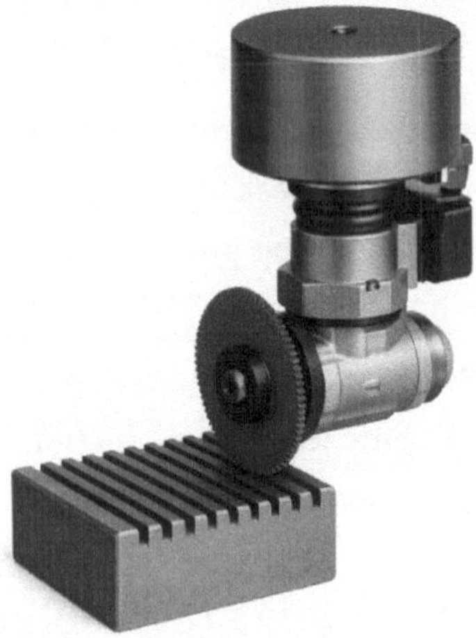

The Results: Dramatic Improvement in Production

- Cycle time reduced by 75%
- Production capacity increased by 300%
- Cutting tool costs have been significantly reduced
- Customer demand met without additional machines, manpower, or capital investment

Key Takeaway: Small Changes, Big Impact

By rethinking tooling strategies and leveraging angular heads, manufacturers can achieve higher efficiency, lower costs, and increased production capacity without expanding their existing setup.

Smart machining solutions = Faster output, lower costs, and higher profits!

CHAPTER 10

Take The Leap

An Invitation to Accelerate Your VMC Productivity

Due to space limitations in this book, I am unable to share all the valuable insights and strategies that can maximize your VMC productivity.

However, my commitment to the machine tool industry and SME business owners remains unwavering.

I strongly believe that SME manufacturers are the backbone of our economy, playing a crucial role in job creation and national stability. My mission is to help grow SME businesses by optimising production by eliminating unnecessary losses so that they can scale efficiently and profitably.

Let's Take It Further – A Personalized Consultation

I invite you to book a one-to-one technical consultancy session with me to gain deeper insights tailored to your specific challenges.

- Identify hidden inefficiencies in your VMC setup
- Explore customized solutions to increase production
- Learn how to reduce costs and maximize ROI
- Discover the latest machining strategies for higher profitability

Your growth is my priority. Let's work together to unlock your VMC's full potential and take your business to the next level!

Reach out to book your consultation today at the link below.